Salads

ACADEMIA BARILLA

The Taunton Press

ACADEMIA BARILLA
AMBASSADOR OF ITALIAN GASTRONOMY
THROUGHOUT THE WORLD

Academia Barilla is a global movement toward the protection, development and promotion of authentic regional Italian culture and cuisine.
With the concept of Food as Culture at our core, Academia Barilla offers a 360° view of Italy. Our comprehensive approach includes:

- a state-of-the-art culinary center in Parma, Italy;
- gourmet travel programs and hands-on cooking classes;
- the world's largest Italian gastronomic library and historic menu collection;
- a portfolio of premium artisan food products;
- global culinary certification programs;
- custom corporate services and training;
- team building activities;
- and a vast assortment of Italian cookbooks.

Thank you and we look forward to welcoming you in Italy soon!

CONTENTS

EDITED BY

ACADEMIA BARILLA

PHOTOGRAPHS

ALBERTO ROSSI

RECIPES BY

CHEF MARIO GRAZIA
CHEF LUCA ZANGA

TEXT BY

MARIAGRAZIA VILLA

ACADEMIA BARILLA EDITORIAL COORDINATION

CHATO MORANDI
ILARIA ROSSI
REBECCA PICKRELL

GRAPHIC DESIGN

PAOLA PIACCO

To make a good salad is to be a brilliant diplomat - the problem is entirely the same in both cases. To know how much oil to mix in with one's vinegar.

OSCAR WILDE, *VERA, OR THE NIHILISTS*, 1880·

SALADS

Experience the magic of a dish rich in aromas, shapes, colors, textures and flavors. With some insight and creativity, you can combine a variety of ingredients to transform your salad into a feast for the senses. An inspired salad can even communicate the joy of sharing a meal together. In Italian cuisine it is considered not only a vegetable dish—whether a single ingredient or mixed ingredients, commonly raw, but also cooked and served cold, to be enjoyed with a dash of salt, oil and vinegar or lemon juice. Salads are also, in the broadest sense, any cold dish seasoned in such a manner and where vegetables may not even be present, or appear only for flavoring or garnish.

Italy's deep appreciation for these ancient dishes goes back to the Romans: even while they enjoyed meats, fish, cheese and bread, they did not neglect the bounty of their vegetable gardens. Indeed, salads—seasoned in a robust, spicy, tangy manner—were served during their banquets to stimulate the appetite. In the Middle Ages, it was meats that were in demand, particularly game, and especially on the tables of the wealthy, but it was with the Renaissance that salads—made from vegetables, enriched with fruits, oil, seeds, flowers, herbs and bold ingredients—re-emerged in vogue, as sumptuous and pivotal creations, the works of great chefs.

As for flavor, the salad is quite easy. But as for the preparation, you need to apply a few tricks to make sure those flavors are blended and balanced. First, consider the combination of ingredients that will go into the salad. For a beginner, it's a good idea to follow a recipe, to prevent the salad from becoming a confused jumble. Then later, with some experience, you can add personal touches—it is important for the ingredients to be able to work with one another in harmony, so that each can draw out the best of the others.

Use a good salad bowl. It should be large and deep enough so that you can easily toss the salad. What material should the utensils be made from? Purists prefer wood, thinking it is the most appropriate for vegetables. Those who are more practical opt for glass or ceramic, because these do not have the drawback of absorbing odors or fats and are not affected by vinegar. Salad servers of glass, bone, or wood are also best.

We have collected 40 salad recipes based on traditions of Italy (or *Bel Paese*, "beautiful country," as Italians call it) and selected by Academia Barilla, the international center dedicated to the preservation and dissemination of Italian gastronomy. We include salads made from vegetables, like the classic Pinzimonio dip, then move on to salads based on rice, grains or pasta, where vegetables, cheeses, legumes and various condiments usually also appear. Then there are salads with chicken, where the meat is boiled and cooled, then cut into small pieces and mixed with other ingredients. Or sometimes fish is the protagonist, like the salad with smoked salmon and fennel; or legumes, as in salads made from chickpeas, beans or fava beans. There are even fruit salads, such as the one from Sicilian cuisine, made from oranges, in which the sauce is savory rather than sweet, created from salt, oil and vinegar or lemon juice.

Of course, if the salad is made from fresh or cooked vegetables, it can act as a side dish to accompany a main course of meat or fish. If it is a mixed salad, including not only vegetables as ingredients, but also proteins such as legumes, cheese, or salami, it can be a delicious appetizer or constitute a refreshing one-course meal, especially in the summer months or at lunchtime. All of the "special" salads, meaning those that contain primarily ingredients besides vegetables, can be served according to what their principal ingredient suggests. For example, a salad of spelt may be enjoyed as a first-course dish, whereas a chicken salad or a tuna salad may be considered a main course. Salads of this type may also be served as appetizers if they are particularly light.

The majority of the salads selected here are Italian by virtue of their creative inspiration and their use of typical regional products. Although some of the preparations offered originate from other culinary regions, like the Salad Niçoise and Greek Salad, they were nonetheless both chosen because they are commonly served in Italian cooking, and also because they share a high quality of raw ingredients, a subtle balance between tradition and innovation and, above all, a convivial spirit. That joy—so contagious and so deeply Italian—makes every salad an event not to be missed.

ORANGE SALAD

Preparation time: 30 minutes   Difficulty: easy

4 SERVINGS

2 **blood oranges**, *preferably Tarocco*
Juice of 1 **lemon**
1 **head endive**
3 1/2 tbsp. (50 ml) **extra-virgin olive oil**
Salt and pepper *to taste*

Cut the peel and white pith from oranges with a sharp knife, then discard.
Cut orange segments free from membranes and, over a bowl, squeeze juice
and reserve the juice.
Whisk the lemon juice with the orange juice, olive oil and a pinch of salt and
pepper. Toss the oranges with the citrus dressing and serve on a bed of endive.

ASPARAGUS SALAD

Preparation time: 25 minutes   Cooking time: 15 minutes   Difficulty: easy

4 SERVINGS

1 lb. (500 g) **asparagus**, *plus 2 stalks more for garnish, if desired*
5 oz. (150 g) **radicchio**, *thinly sliced*
1 oz. (30 g) **radishes**, *thinly sliced*
1/3 cup (80 ml) **extra-virgin olive oil**
Salt and pepper *to taste*

Wash the asparagus and cut to equal lengths. Peel the fibrous ends.
Tie the asparagus into bunches and boil in salted water, with the tips upward to prevent breaking, until cooked but still firm, 10-15 minutes. Drain, cool and cut lengthwise into halves. Season with salt and pepper, and drizzle with oil. Season radicchio with salt and pepper, then drizzle with oil. Arrange the asparagus and radicchio on individual plates, then garnish with radishes and thin-sliced asparagus, if desired.

AVOCADO, ORANGE, MELON
AND STRAWBERRY SALAD

Preparation time: 20 minutes   Difficulty: easy

4 SERVINGS

2 avocados
2 oranges
1/2 melon
4 1/2 oz. (125 g) strawberries
7 oz. (200 g) plain yogurt
Lemon juice *to taste*
Salt and green pepper *to taste, or 1 tsp. sugar (optional)*

Wash, peel and halve the avocados. Remove the pits and then cube. Wash, dry and cut the melon in half again. Remove the seeds from the melon and finely cube.
Remove the orange peels and pith enclosing the orange segments. Halve the segments. Delicately wash and dry the strawberries, then cut into small pieces. Squeeze a few drops of lemon juice into the yogurt and stir to combine. Season with salt and green pepper; or for a sweeter version, season with sugar instead. Drizzle with yogurt dressing.

CABBAGE SALAD
WITH DRIED APRICOTS AND HAZELNUTS

Preparation time: 20 minutes *Difficulty: easy*

4 SERVINGS

3/4 lb. (300 g) **cabbage** *(round, smooth-leaved variety)*
1/4 lb. (100 g) **dried apricots**
2 oz. (60 g) **toasted hazelnuts**, *or about 1/2 cup*
1/3 cup plus 1 1/2 tbsp. (100 ml) **extra-virgin olive oil**
2 tbsp. (30 ml) **white wine vinegar**
Salt and freshly ground pepper *to taste (optional)*

Remove the outer leaves of the cabbage and discard; cut cabbage into thin strips, then wash well and drain. Coarsely chop the hazelnuts and cut the dried apricots into strips. (If the apricots are very dry, you can plump them in water for about 10 minutes.)
Whisk together the olive oil and vinegar, salt and, if desired, freshly ground pepper. Drizzle the dressing over the cabbage, add the apricots and hazelnuts, then toss and serve.

ZESTY CITRUS CHICKPEA SALAD

Preparation time: 20 minutes   Difficulty: easy

4 SERVINGS

1 lb. (500 g) **cooked chickpeas**, *drained twice*
2 tsp. (10 g) **lemon zest**, *minced*
2 tsp. (10 g) **orange zest**, *minced*
2 tsp. (10 g) **lime zest**, *minced*
1/2 (75 g) **yellow bell pepper**, *finely cubed*
1/4 (50 g) **red bell pepper**, *finely cubed*
1/4 (50 g) **red onion**, *finely cubed*
1/4 **green apple**, *finely cubed*
1/3 cup (80 ml) **extra-virgin olive oil**
1 tbsp. (15 ml) **wine vinegar**
Salt and pepper *to taste*

Mix together chickpeas, zests, bell peppers, red onion and apple. Drizzle with olive oil and vinegar and season with salt and pepper. Toss until combined.

SALAD OF BEAN SPROUTS, CARROTS AND WATERMELON

Preparation time: 20 minutes   Difficulty: easy

4 SERVINGS

5 oz. (150 g) **bean sprouts**
7 oz. (200 g) **carrots**
12 1/2 oz. (350 g) **watermelon**
3 1/2 tbsp. (50 ml) **soy sauce**
3 1/2 tbsp. (50 ml) **extra-virgin olive oil**

Peel the carrots. Cut into thin strips using a mandoline or vegetable peeler, then place in ice water for about 10 minutes. Drain just before mixing with other ingredients.
Remove the rind and seeds of the watermelon, then cube.
Rinse the bean sprouts and drain on a cloth with the carrots.
Mix together the carrots, watermelon and bean sprouts, and arrange in a bowl or in 4 individual bowls. Toss lightly with soy sauce and a drizzle of olive oil. Serve.

FRESH VEGETABLE
AND CORN SALAD

Preparation time: 10 minutes   Difficulty: easy

4 SERVINGS

1 16-oz. can **corn**
10 1/2 oz. (300 g) **bell pepper**, *or about 2 medium, finely diced*
3 1/2 oz. (100 g) **cucumber**, *finely diced*
2 1/2 oz. (70 g) **celery**, *finely diced*
2 oz. (60 g) **spring onion**, *thinly sliced*
1 3/4 oz. (50 g) **pitted olives**, *chopped*
1/3 cup plus 1 1/2 tbsp. (100 ml) **extra-virgin olive oil**
3/4 cup (20 g) **chopped parsley**
Salt and pepper *to taste*

Mix together all the vegetables and olives with olive oil. Season with salt and
pepper and garnish with the parsley. Serve.

GREEN OLIVE SALAD

Preparation time: 15 minutes   Difficulty: easy

4 SERVINGS

14 oz. (400 g) **pitted green olives**, *preferably Sicilian olives from Belice*
3 1/2 oz. (100 g) **celery**
1 tbsp. plus 1 tsp. (20 ml) **extra-virgin olive oil**
5 **fresh mint leaves**, *thinly sliced*
2 tsp. (10 ml) **white wine vinegar**
Salt *to taste*
Red chile pepper *(fresh), sliced (optional)*

Crush the olives and rinse under running water. Place them in a salad bowl, add the celery and mint leaves, and toss with oil, vinegar and salt. If desired, garnish with chile-pepper slices.

POTATO SALAD

Preparation time: 20 minutes   Difficulty: easy

4-6 SERVINGS

1 1/3 lbs. (600 g) **yellow, white and purple potatoes**, boiled with the skins on
1/3 cup plus 1 1/2 tbsp. (100 ml) **plain yogurt**
1/3 cup plus 1 1/2 tbsp. (100 ml) **extra-virgin olive oil**
Fresh chives, for garnish
Salt to taste

Peel the boiled potatoes and cut them into 3/4-inch cubes; transfer to a bowl.
Mix the yogurt with the olive oil and a pinch of salt.
Toss the potatoes with the dressing. Arrange the salad on a serving plate,
garnish with strands of chives and serve.

CELERY ROOT, RADICCHIO AND PINEAPPLE SALAD

Preparation time: 30 minutes   Difficulty: easy

4 SERVINGS

10 1/2 oz. (300 g) **celery root**
3 1/2 oz. (100 g) **radicchio**
1/2 **fresh pineapple**, peeled and cubed
1 **lemon**
1/4 cup (60 ml) **extra-virgin olive oil**
3/4 cup (20 g) **chopped fresh parsley** (optional)
Salt and pepper to taste

Peel and thinly slice the celery root; then cut into strips and soak in cold water with the juice of the lemon until ready to mix and serve. Drain celery root. Blend a quarter of the pineapple with the olive oil in a blender and season with salt and pepper.

Mix the celery root with the remaining pineapple. Serve on beds of radicchio and drizzle with pineapple dressing. If desired, garnish with parsley.

PINK GRAPEFRUIT, SPINACH
AND WALNUT SALAD

Preparation time: 20 minutes   Difficulty: easy

4 SERVINGS

2 pink grapefruits
2 oranges
2 lemons
7 oz. (200 g) **baby spinach**
3 1/2 oz. (100 g) **chopped walnuts** *(1 cup)*
1/3 cup plus 1 1/2 tbsp. (100 ml) **extra-virgin olive oil**
Salt and pepper *to taste*

Remove the peel and pith from the oranges and lemon. Working over a bowl to catch the juices, use a paring knife to slice between the sections and membranes of each fruit; remove the segments whole, reserving the fruit and juice.
Whisk the juice with the olive oil and a pinch of salt and pepper.
On individual plates, arrange the spinach and the fruit segments. Drizzle with the dressing and garnish with walnuts.

SEASONAL SALAD
IN CRUNCHY BREAD BASKETS

Preparation time: 30 minutes   Difficulty: easy

4 SERVINGS

3 oz. (100 g) **mixed salad greens**
3 oz. (100 g) **boiled green beans**, *chopped*
1 **fennel**, *diced small*
1 **cucumber**
1 lb. (500 g) **rustic bread**, *preferably pane di Altamura (bread from Altamura, made from semolina flour)*
2 tbsp. **white wine vinegar**
1 tbsp. **balsamic vinegar**
2 tbsp. **extra-virgin olive oil**
Salt and pepper *to taste*

Preheat oven to 350°F (180°C). Peel the cucumber, scoop out the seeds, and cut the cucumber into cubes. Transfer the cucumber to a colander, lightly salt, and let drain.
Meanwhile, cut the rustic bread (pane di Altamura) into 12 thin slices, then line at least 4 single-serving aluminum molds with slices. Lightly oil the bread and place the molds in the oven, and toast the bread until crunchy baskets form, 2 to 3 minutes. Let cool.
Meanwhile, place the mixed salad greens, green beans, fennel and cucumber in a bowl. Drizzle the salad with white wine vinegar and balsamic vinegar, and season with salt and pepper; mix well. Remove the breadbaskets from the molds, arrange the salad in the baskets of bread and serve.

ZUCCHINI SALAD WITH MINT

Preparation time: 10 minutes   Marinating time: 30 minutes   Difficulty: easy

4 SERVINGS

14 oz. (400 g) **zucchini**
5 oz. (150 g) **radicchio**
1/4 cup (60 ml) **extra-virgin olive oil**
1 **bunch fresh mint**
1 clove **garlic**
Salt and pepper *to taste*

Gently heat the olive oil in a pan. Turn off the heat and add the garlic and a few whole mint leaves until oil is infused, about 30 minutes.
Cut the zucchini in half and remove the seeds, then slice zucchini into matchsticks.
On a plate, arrange a bed of radicchio and the zucchini matchsticks. Drizzle with the flavored oil, season with salt and pepper, then garnish with the mint leaves.

SUMMER SALAD
WITH ITALIAN BUTTER BEANS

Preparation time: 30 minutes   Difficulty: easy

4 SERVINGS

1/2 lb. (250 g) **Italian butter beans** *or gigante beans, boiled*
7 oz. (200 g) **cucumber**
1 **celery heart**, *chopped*
4 **small tomatoes**, *cut into rounds*
1 **sprig wild fennel**
5 oz. (150 g) **salad greens**, *torn into large pieces*
Juice of 1 **lemon**
1/3 cup (80 ml) **extra-virgin olive oil**
Salt and freshly ground pepper *to taste*
Fresh chives, *for garnish (optional)*

Place lemon juice, olive oil, pinch of salt and the fennel in a blender and blend until mixture reaches consistency of a smooth sauce. Cut the cucumbers into half lengthwise, scoop out the seeds and slice cucumber into half-rounds.
In a bowl, combine the cucumbers, butter beans and celery heart; then season everything with half of the prepared sauce, mixing thoroughly.
Place the salad greens along the bottom of a serving dish and top with butter bean salad. Garnish with the tomatoes and fresh chives, if desired. Drizzle with the remaining sauce. Season generously with freshly ground pepper and serve.

MIXED SALAD
WITH PINEAPPLE AND MELON

Preparation time: 30 minutes   Difficulty: easy

4 SERVINGS

7 oz. (200 g) **green beans**
1 **pineapple**
1 **cantaloupe melon**
12 **cherry tomatoes**
1 **green bell pepper**
Juice of 1 **lemon**
1 tbsp. (4 g) **chopped fresh parsley**
Tabasco sauce *to taste*
1/3 cup (80 ml) **extra-virgin olive oil**
Salt *to taste*

Cut the melon in half. Peel and cube one half. Cut the other half, peel still on, into very thin slices.

Peel the pineapple and cut into fairly large pieces. Bring water to a boil in a saucepan, and cook the green beans to crisp-tender. Coarsely chop the boiled green beans and the bell pepper. Cut the tomatoes into quarters. Mix fruits and vegetables together in a large bowl.

Blend the olive oil, lemon juice, Tabasco sauce, a pinch of salt and parsley to create a citronette dressing. On the individual plates, arrange the salad and drizzle with the dressing. Garnish with parsley.

MIXED SALAD
WITH GREEN BEANS

Preparation time: 20 minutes   Difficulty: easy

6 SERVINGS

1 pound (500 g) **green beans**, *boiled*
5 oz. (150 g) **red and yellow bell peppers**, *thinly sliced*
Extra-virgin olive oil
1 **stalk celery**, *finely chopped*
2 tbsp. (30 ml) **balsamic vinegar**
3/4 tsp. (4 g) **mustard**
1 **hard-boiled egg**, *yolk only*
Salt *to taste*

In a bowl, use a whisk to mix the yolk, mustard, balsamic vinegar and a pinch of salt. Slowly drizzle in extra-virgin olive oil until the dressing is emulsified. On individual plates, arrange the green beans, celery and bell peppers, drizzle with dressing, and serve.

PINZIMONIO (VEGETABLE DIP)

Preparation time: 10 minutes   *Difficulty: easy*

4 SERVINGS

2 carrots
2 celery stalks
1/2 yellow bell pepper
1/2 red bell pepper
1/2 green bell pepper
2 green onions
1 cucumber
Extra-virgin olive oil
Balsamic vinegar
Salt and pepper

Wash and clean the vegetables. Remove the seeds from the cucumber and bell peppers. Cut all the vegetables into matchsticks of equal length and place on a serving dish or in 4 individual cups.
Prepare 4 small dipping bowls of olive oil for each guest. Arrange salt, pepper and balsamic vinegar at the center of the table, so each guest can season, as desired.

FAVA BEANS
WITH PORK CHEEK

Preparation time: 30 minutes   Cooking time: 15 minutes   Difficulty: easy

4 SERVINGS

2 1/4 lb. (1 kg) **fresh fava beans** *(broad beans)*
2 2/3 oz. (75 g) **pork cheek (guanciale)**, *cut into thin slivers*
1 **small onion**, *chopped*
2 tbsp. (30 ml) **extra-virgin olive oil**
Salt and pepper *to taste*

In a saucepan (preferably earthenware), sauté the onion and pork cheek in the
olive oil. When the pork and the onion have browned slightly, add the fava
beans and salt and pepper, to taste, and continue to cook. Add warm water
occasionally, if necessary, and serve hot.
(If you use dried fava beans that have already been boiled, reduce the cooking
time and add a little dry white wine during cooking.)

RADICCHIO WITH SPECK

Preparation time: 15 minutes   Difficulty: easy

4 SERVINGS

2 heads **radicchio**
7 oz. (200 g) **speck**, or smoked bacon, cut into slivers
2 tbsp. (30 ml) **balsamic vinegar**
2 tbsp. (30 ml) **olive oil**
Salt and pepper to taste

In a pan, sauté the speck in olive oil. When the speck is golden brown, add the balsamic vinegar and let it evaporate. Drizzle the pan sauce on the radicchio, season with salt and pepper and toss. Serve immediately.

APPLE, CHICKEN
AND TOASTED-FOCACCIA SALAD

Preparation time: 30 minutes   Cooking time: 20 minutes   Difficulty: easy

4 SERVINGS

3 **green apples**, 2 cubed and 1 thinly sliced for garnish
7 oz. (200 g) **radicchio**, thinly sliced
10 1/2 oz. (300 g) **chicken breast**
3 1/2 oz. (100 g) **focaccia**
1/4 cup (20 g) **sliced almonds**
1/3 cup plus 1 1/2 tbsp. (100 ml) **extra-virgin olive oil**
1 tbsp. plus 1 tsp. (20 ml) **vinegar**
Salt and pepper to taste

Preheat oven to 350°F (180°C). Season chicken with salt and pepper, then drizzle with olive oil. Bake chicken until cooked through, 18 to 20 minutes (alternatively, you can grill it). Let cool, then cut into cubes.

Cut the focaccia into cubes and toast in the oven for 5 minutes.

Toss radicchio with olive oil and vinegar and season with salt and pepper. Add the apples, chicken, focaccia and almonds and serve in individual bowls. Garnish with apple slices.

CHICKEN SALAD
WITH BALSAMIC VINEGAR AND PINE NUTS

Preparation time: 15 minutes   Cooking time: 20 minutes   Difficulty: easy

4 SERVINGS

14 oz. (400 g) **chicken breast**, *cleaned and separated*
1 3/4 oz. (50 g) **pine nuts** *(about 3/4 cup)*
3 1/2 oz. (100 g) **arugula**
3/4 cup plus 2 1/4 tbsp. (200 ml) **balsamic vinegar**
1 1/2 cups (350 ml) **water**

1/3 cup plus 1 1/2 tbsp. (100 ml) **extra-virgin olive oil**
2 **sprigs of sage**
2 **sprigs of rosemary**
1 **bay leaf**
1 clove **garlic**
Salt and pepper *to taste*

Chop half of the herbs. In a saucepan, over medium heat, put 1/2 cup plus 2 1/2 tablespoons of balsamic vinegar, a little salt and the unchopped herbs and cover with water. Bring to a boil and add the chicken breasts. Cook for about 20 minutes, then let the chicken cool in the liquid.

Slice the chicken breast and allow to marinate with oil and the chopped herbs for about 15 minutes. In a skillet, over medium heat, toast the pine nuts, taking care not to let them become too dark. In a bowl, emulsify the remaining balsamic vinegar with the olive oil and a pinch of salt and pepper.

Toss arugula with vinegar-and-oil dressing, then arrange arugula on individual plates with slices of chicken on top. Sprinkle with toasted pine nuts. Finish with a few more drops of the dressing.

VEAL SALAD
WITH HONEY-SESAME DRESSING

Preparation time: 20 minutes   Difficulty: easy

4 SERVINGS

5 oz. (150 g) **celery**, *thinly sliced*
5 oz. (150 g) **carrots**, *thinly sliced*
14 oz. (400 g) **roast veal**, *cold*
1 oz. (30 g) **radishes**, *thinly sliced*
3/4 cup (20 g) **chopped fresh parsley**
1/3 cup (80 ml) **extra-virgin olive oil**
2 tbsp. plus 2 tsp. (40 g) **honey**
2 tbsp. (25 g) **mustard**
2 tsp. (10 g) **sesame seeds**
Salt and pepper *to taste*

Cut the cold roast veal into pieces. Mix the meat with the vegetables, then toss
with salt, pepper, parsley and half of the olive oil.
In a pan, over medium heat, toast the sesame seeds, then allow them to cool.
Blend together the sesame seeds, honey, mustard and the remaining olive oil in
a blender. Season with salt. On individual plates, arrange the salads and drizzle
with the honey-sesame dressing.

MIXED SALAD GREENS
WITH SPECK AND RASPBERRIES

Preparation time: 15 minutes   Difficulty: easy

4 SERVINGS

7 oz. (200 g) **mixed salad greens**
5 oz. (150 g) **speck**
2 oz. (60 g) **raspberries**, *or about 1/2 cup*
3 1/2 tbsp. (50 ml) **extra-virgin olive oil**
1 tbsp. (15 ml) **raspberry-flavored vinegar**
Salt and pepper *to taste*

Cut half the speck into very thin slices and the remaining half into
very thin batons.
Arrange the mixed salad greens on individual plates with the batons
of speck mixed in. Surround the salad with the thin slices of speck and garnish
with the raspberries.
In a bowl, whisk together the olive oil, vinegar, salt and pepper. Drizzle
dressing over the salad.

CAPONATA WITH MACKEREL

Preparation time: 20 minutes   Difficulty: easy

4 SERVINGS

4 crisp round bread croutons
7 oz. (200 g) boiled mackerel
14 oz. (400 g) cauliflower
5 oz. (150 g) pickled mixed vegetables
(giardiniera), chopped
2 pickled Neapolitan peppers,
chopped
1 head escarole, chopped
1 head lettuce, chopped

3 1/2 oz. (100 g) capers
3 1/2 oz. (100 g) pitted black olives
4 salted anchovies, chopped
7 tbsp. (100 g) extra-virgin olive oil
7 tbsp. (100 g) white vinegar
7 tbsp. (100 g) white wine
Lemon juice to taste
Salt and pepper to taste

Boil the cauliflower in water with salt and lemon juice until tender.
Combine it in a large salad bowl with the anchovies, pickled vegetables, pickled
Neapolitan peppers, escarole and lettuce, plus the capers and olives. Season
with a pinch of salt and pepper. Drizzle with oil and vinegar, and mix well.
In a container, soak the "freselle" (crisp round bread croutons) in the vinegar and
wine; once softened, coarsely crumble into the salad bowl and mix well, leveling
off the top. Arrange the mackerel on top. Drizzle with lemon juice.

SMOKED SALMON
WITH FENNEL SALAD

Preparation time: 30 minutes   Difficulty: easy

4 SERVINGS

1 lb. (450 g) **fennel,** *finely sliced (greens reserved for garnish)*
7 oz. (200 g) **smoked salmon**
2 **lemons**
1/3 cup plus 1 1/2 tbsp. (100 ml) **extra-virgin olive oil**
Salt and pepper *to taste*

Slice the salmon and arrange on a plate. Drizzle with the juice of 1 lemon and
allow to marinate for about 10 minutes.
Meanwhile, in a bowl, whisk the juice of remaining lemon, the olive oil, salt and
pepper. Drizzle some dressing over the fennel.
Arrange the fennel salad on individual plates and cover with slices of salmon.
Drizzle with the remaining dressing and garnish with the fennel greens.

TUNA SALAD WITH BEANS

Preparation time: 1 1/2 hours   Soaking time: 12 hours   Difficulty: medium

4 SERVINGS

7 oz. (200 g) **baby lettuce**
5 oz. (150 g) **dried cannellini beans**
5 oz. (150 g) **canned tuna in oil**, *drained*
1/3 **red bell pepper**, *thinly sliced*
7 oz. (200 g) **red onion**, *sliced into rings*
1/3 cup plus 1 1/2 tbsp. (100 ml) **extra-virgin olive oil**
Salt and freshly ground pepper *to taste*

Soak the beans in cold water for at least 12 hours. Boil in unsalted water until tender, about an hour. Allow beans to cool, then drain. Drizzle with olive oil and season with salt.

Arrange a bed of lettuce on individual plates and top with layers of beans, onion and tuna. Garnish with bell pepper and some freshly ground pepper.

MIMOSA SALAD WITH TROUT

Preparation time: 50 minutes   Cooking time: 10 minutes   Difficulty: easy

4 SERVINGS

4 *eggs*
14 oz. (400 g) *potatoes*
3 1/2 oz. (100 g) *mixed salad greens*
14 oz. (400 g) *trout fillet*
1/3 cup (40 g) *chopped walnuts*
1/3 cup plus 1 1/2 tbsp. (100 ml) **extra-virgin olive oil**
Juice from 1 **lemon**
Salt and pepper *to taste*

Place the eggs in a saucepan, cover with water, and bring to a boil.
Allow to boil for 8 to 10 minutes. Drain the eggs and immediately submerge them in cold water to stop the cooking process (and make them easier to peel). Shell the eggs. After peeling, separate the yolks from the whites (which are not used in this recipe). Heat oven to 350°F (180°C).
Wash the potatoes and boil, unpeeled, in a pot of salted water for about 10 minutes. Drain, cool, peel and cut into wedges, about 1/4 inch thick.
Carefully remove any bones from the trout fillets. Season with pepper and arrange on a baking sheet greased with a little oil. Bake for 8 to 10 minutes. Allow to cool and remove the skin.
Toss the mixed salad greens in olive oil, lemon juice and a pinch of salt. Arrange beds of greens on individual plates and top with the potatoes and trout. Drizzle everything with more oil, lemon juice and a pinch of salt. Press the hard-boiled egg yolks through a sieve and sprinkle over the salad. Garnish with a few walnuts.

SALAD NIÇOISE

Preparation time: 1 hour   Cooking time: 20 minutes   Difficulty: easy

4 SERVINGS

4 **eggs**
14 oz. (400 g) **potatoes**
3 1/2 oz. (100 g) **lettuce**
10 1/2 oz. (300 g) **green beans**
14 oz. (400 g) **tomatoes**, cut into wedges
10 1/2 oz. (300 g) **tuna (in oil)**, flaked into large chunks

1 3/4 oz. (50 g) **pitted black olives**
4 **salted anchovies**, filleted
1/3 cup plus 1 1/2 tbsp. (100 ml) **extra-virgin olive oil**
1 tsp. **mustard**
1 1/2 tbsp. (25 ml) **red wine vinegar**
Salt and pepper to taste
Fresh basil leaves for garnish (optional)

Place the eggs in a saucepan, cover with water, and bring to a boil. Allow to boil for 8-10 minutes. Drain the eggs and immediately submerge them in cold water to stop the cooking process (and make them easier to peel). Peel the eggs and cut into wedges.

Boil potatoes, with skins on, in a pot of salted water, just until tender, 10 to 15 minutes; then drain, cool, peel and cut into wedges. Toss with salt, pepper, a dash of vinegar and a drizzle of olive oil.

Trim and boil the green beans in salted water, then drain and refresh immediately in iced water to stop the cooking and retain the color.

For the vinaigrette dressing, whisk the remaining oil with the red wine vinegar, the mustard, salt and pepper.

On individual plates, arrange a bed of lettuce and top with potatoes and green beans. Surround these with the wedges of hard-cooked eggs, alternating with tomato wedges and chunks of tuna. Garnish with anchovy fillets and olives, then drizzle with the vinaigrette.

GREEK SALAD

Preparation time: 10 minutes Difficulty: easy

4 SERVINGS

3 **tomatoes**, *sliced, or 10 oz. cherry tomatoes, halved*
1 **red onion**, *thinly sliced*
2 **cucumbers**, *cubed*
7 oz. (200 g) **feta cheese**, *cubed*
1/3 cup plus 1 1/2 tbsp. (100 ml) **extra-virgin olive oil**
1 3/4 oz. (50 g) **Greek olives**
Pinch of **oregano** *(optional)*
Salt *to taste*

Place the tomatoes, cucumbers, feta, onions and olives in a large bowl. Drizzle with olive oil and gently toss. Season with salt. Garnish with oregano, if desired.

ARTICHOKE SALAD
WITH PARMIGIANO-REGGIANO

Preparation time: 20 minutes   Difficulty: easy

4 SERVINGS

4 **artichokes**
1 cup plus 3 tbsp. (120 g) **Parmigiano-Reggiano cheese**
Juice of 2 **lemons**, plus zest for garnish, if desired
4-5 **fresh mint leaves**
3 1/2 tbsp. (50 ml) **extra-virgin olive oil**, preferably Ligurian
Salt and pepper to taste

Clean the artichokes, removing the outer leaves and spines.
Clean the stems and soak them in a mixture of water and lemon juice for 15 minutes. Grate or slice the Parmigiano into thin pieces.
Whisk together the lemon juice, olive oil and a pinch of salt and pepper.
Cut the artichokes in half, removing any tough inner fibers, and scoop out fuzzy choke with a melon-ball cutter.
Just before serving, slice artichokes paper-thin crosswise (you can use a Japanese Benriner or other adjustable-blade slicer). Drizzle the artichokes with the lemon and olive oil emulsion.
Arrange the artichokes in the center of the plates.
Top them with Parmigiano slices, mint leaves and a drizzle of olive oil. Garnish with lemon zest, if desired.

ASSORTED CHEESE SALAD

Preparation time: 20 minutes   Difficulty: easy

4 SERVINGS

3 1/2 oz. (100 g) **Gruyère cheese**, *cut into matchsticks*

3 1/2 oz. (100 g) **Provolone cheese**, *cut into matchsticks*

3 1/2 oz. (100 g) **Caciocavallo or provolone cheese**, *cut into matchsticks*

3 1/2 oz. (100 g) **Asiago cheese**, *cut into matchsticks*

3 1/2 oz. (100 g) **radicchio**, *thinly sliced*

3 oz. (80 g) **celery**, *thinly sliced*

1 3/4 oz. (50 g) **radishes**, *thinly sliced*

1/3 cup (10 g) **chives**, *finely chopped*

FOR THE DRESSING
1/3 cup (80 g) **mayonnaise**
1/2 cup (125 g) **plain yogurt**
Salt *to taste*
or
1/3 cup (80 ml) **extra-virgin olive oil**
1 1/2 tbsp. (25 ml) **balsamic vinegar**
Salt *to taste*

In a bowl, mix everything together, then pour the mayonnaise, yogurt and pinch of salt over the cheese salad. Alternatively, drizzle the olive oil and balsamic vinegar with a pinch of salt over the cheese salad—or serve the dressing on the side.

PECORINO SALAD
WITH FAVA BEANS AND PARMA HAM

Preparation time: 20 minutes   Cooking time: 10 minutes   Difficulty: easy

4 SERVINGS

1 1/3 lbs. (600 g) **fresh fava beans**
7 oz. (200 g) **sliced Parma ham** (prosciutto di Parma)
7 oz. (200 g) **medium-aged pecorino cheese**
3 1/2 oz. (100 g) **mixed salad leaves**
1 tbsp. (15 ml) **wine vinegar**
1/4 cup (60 ml) **extra-virgin olive oil**
Salt to taste

Bring a pot of salted water to a boil. Shell the beans and cook in the boiling water for about 10 minutes.
Drain, cool and remove the skins. Place in a bowl and add a drizzle of extra-virgin olive oil and a pinch of salt.
Thinly slice the Pecorino using a mandoline or similar tool.
Drizzle the mixed salad greens with the remaining olive oil, the vinegar and a pinch of salt. Layer the fava beans, the pecorino and the slices of Parma ham on top of the greens and serve.

GRAIN SALAD
WITH HERBS AND VEGETABLES

Preparation time: 15 minutes   Cooking time: 45 minutes   Difficulty: easy

4 SERVINGS

2 1/2 oz. (70 g) **rice**
2 1/2 oz. (70 g) **barley**
2 1/2 oz. (70 g) **spelt**
1/4 cup (60 ml) **extra-virgin olive oil**
1 3/4 (50 g) **celery**, *diced*
3 1/2 oz. (100 g) **leeks**, *sliced (white part only)*
7 oz. (200 g) **eggplant**
3 1/2 oz. (100 g) **zucchini**, *diced*
3 1/2 oz. (100 g) **red bell pepper**,

diced
3 1/2 oz. (100 g) **yellow bell pepper**, *diced*
5 oz. (150 g) **carrots**, *diced*
2 **sprigs thyme**, *chopped, plus 4 springs thyme for garnish (optional)*
2 **sprigs marjoram**, *chopped*
2 **sprigs sage**, *chopped*
2 **sprigs rosemary**, *chopped*
Salt *to taste*

Boil separately in salted water the rice, barley and spelt (for an alternative, to speed preparation, you can use a mix of precooked grains). Drain while still al dente and let cool, spreading out in a baking pan and stirring occasionally. Meanwhile, cube the eggplant, lightly salt it and allow to drain in a colander for about 30 minutes.

In a pan, sauté each of the vegetables separately with a little oil and the chopped herbs until crisp-tender. Season with salt, then add to a bowl with the grains. Drizzle with the remaining extra-virgin olive oil and add salt to taste.

MARGHERITA-STYLE
PASTA SALAD

Preparation time: 15 minutes   Cooking time: 8 minutes   Difficulty: easy

4 SERVINGS

12 oz. (320 g) **shell-shaped pasta**
8 3/4 oz. (250 g) **mozzarella**
2 **tomatoes** *or 7 oz.* **cherry tomatoes**
4-5 **fresh basil leaves**
1/3 cup (80 ml) **extra-virgin olive oil**
Salt *to taste*

Boil the pasta in a pot of salted water until al dente. Remove from heat and quickly rinse under cold running water, then carefully drain.
Transfer pasta to a large bowl and toss with a drizzle of olive oil so that it does not stick together. Cut the tomatoes and the mozzarella into 1/4-inch cubes and mix together with the pasta in the large bowl. Toss with olive oil and basil. Season with salt. Serve.

BOWTIE PASTA SALAD
WITH MELON BALLS

Preparation time: 25 minutes   Cooking time: 12 minutes   Difficulty: easy

4 SERVINGS

7 oz. (200 g) **bowtie pasta (farfalle)**
2 **cantaloupe melons**, *halved and seeded*
1 **bell pepper**, *finely diced*
1 **zucchini**, *finely diced*
5 oz. (150 g) **carrots**, *finely diced*
2 cups (50 g) **fresh parsley**, *chopped*
1/4 cup (60 ml) **extra-virgin olive oil**
Salt *to taste*

Boil the pasta in a pot of salted water until al dente. Remove from heat and quickly rinse under cold running water, then carefully drain.
Transfer to a large bowl and toss with a drizzle of olive oil so it does not stick together.
Make melon balls with a melon baller, reserving the melon shells for serving.
Combine all the vegetables with the pasta. Add the melon balls, parsley, salt to taste and olive oil. Mix thoroughly and serve the salad in the melon shells.

FUSILLI PASTA SALAD
WITH ASPARAGUS AND PARMA HAM

Preparation time: 30 minutes   Cooking time: 13 minutes   Difficulty: easy

4 SERVINGS

10 1/2 oz. (300 g) **fusilli-type pasta**
3 1/2 tbsp. (50 g) **butter**
4 1/2 oz. (130 g) **Parma ham** (prosciutto di Parma), *cut into wide strips*
7 oz. (200 g) **asparagus**
3 1/2 tbsp. (50 ml) **extra-virgin olive oil**
3/4 cup (20 g) **chopped fresh parsley**
1 clove **garlic**
Zest of 1 **lemon**, *cut into thin strips*
Salt and pepper *to taste*

Boil the pasta in a pot of salted water until al dente. Remove from heat and quickly rinse under cold running water, then carefully drain. Transfer to a large bowl and toss with a drizzle of olive oil so it does not stick together.
Peel the fibrous ends of the asparagus, then cut into rounds, keeping the tips whole. Place in a pan with half the butter and the garlic, and allow to simmer for about 10 minutes over medium heat.
Meanwhile, in a pan, sauté the ham with the remaining butter, without letting it go dry. Moisten with a ladleful of water and add the asparagus. Season with salt and pepper. Add the asparagus and ham to the pasta and mix well. Garnish with a little lemon zest and chopped parsley. Drizzle with extra-virgin olive oil.

SARDINIAN-STYLE PASTA SALAD
WITH TUNA, ZUCCHINI AND BELL PEPPERS

Preparation time: 30 minutes   Cooking time: 13 minutes   Difficulty: easy

4 SERVINGS

10 1/2 oz. (300 g) **gnocchetti sardi**
(malloreddus) or cavatelli
14 oz. (400 g) **fresh tuna steak**
10 1/2 oz. (300 g) **round zucchini** (such
as globe squash), finely cubed
1 **red bell pepper**, finely cubed
1 **yellow bell pepper**, finely cubed

3 1/2 oz. (100 g) **fresh fava beans**
3 oz. (80 g) **peas**
1/3 cup plus 1 1/2 tbsp. (100 ml) **extra-
virgin olive oil**
Lemon juice to taste
Salt and pepper to taste

Boil the pasta in a pot of salted water until al dente. Remove from heat and quickly rinse under cold running water, then carefully drain. Transfer to a large bowl and toss with a drizzle of olive oil so it does not stick together.
Separately blanch the peas and beans in salted boiling water for a couple of minutes, then transfer immediately to ice water to refresh. Peel the beans.
Sauté the vegetables with one third of the olive oil until crisp-tender, then season with salt and pepper. Season the tuna with salt and pepper and drizzle with remaining olive oil; then grill on a hot griddle (or a nonstick pan) until cooked through but still pink, a couple of minutes per side.
Add all the vegetables to the pasta and mix well, adding the remaining oil. Finally, cube the tuna steak and add to the pasta mix. Drizzle with a few drops of lemon juice.

WHOLE-GRAIN PASTA SALAD
WITH AVOCADO, CHICKEN, CHERRY TOMATOES AND CORN

Preparation time: 20 minutes   Cooking time: 20 minutes   Difficulty: easy

4 SERVINGS

10 1/2 oz. (300 g) **whole-grain penne**
5 oz. (150 g) **cherry tomatoes**, *halved*
5 oz. (150 g) **chicken breast**
2 **avocados**, *halved and pitted (reserving shells for serving, if desired)*
3/4 cup (20 g) **fresh chopped parsley**
5 oz. (150 g) **corn** *(canned or frozen)*
1/4 cup (60 ml) **extra-virgin olive oil**
Salt and pepper *to taste*

Preheat oven to 350°F (180°C). Season the chicken breast with salt and pepper.
Drizzle with extra-virgin olive oil, then bake until cooked through, 18 to 20
minutes (alternatively, grill it). Let cool, then cut into cubes.
Meanwhile, boil the pasta in a pot of salted water until al dente. Remove from
heat and quickly rinse under cold running water, then carefully drain.
Using a melon baller, form avocado into small balls, or cut into cubes.
Combine the pasta with chicken, tomatoes, avocados, and corn. Season with salt,
then add olive oil and parsley. Mix thoroughly and serve in hollow avocado shells.

SPRING RICE SALAD

Preparation time: 25 minutes   Cooking time: 15 minutes   Difficulty: easy

4 SERVINGS

7 oz. (200 g) **rice**
4 oz. (120 g) **peas**
5 oz. (150 g) **asparagus**
1 3/4 oz. (50 g) **squash blossoms,** *cut into strips*
1/3 cup plus 1 1/2 tbsp. (100 ml) **extra-virgin olive oil**
Salt *to taste*

Add the rice to boiling salted water and cook for about 15 minutes, or following package instructions. Meanwhile, boil the peas for a couple of minutes, in salted water, then immediately transfer to ice water.
Wash the asparagus and peel the fibrous ends. Trim to equal lengths.
Tie into bunches and boil in salted water, with the tips upward to prevent breaking, until cooked but still firm, 10 to 15 minutes.
When the rice is ready, drain the rice and quickly rinse under cold running water and transfer to a bowl. Add the prepared ingredients. Season with a pinch of salt and drizzle with olive oil. Stir the rice salad well and serve cold.

SEDANINI PASTA SALAD
WITH GREEN APPLES, RAISINS AND ALMONDS

Preparation time: 30 minutes   Cooking time: 13 minutes   Difficulty: easy

4 SERVINGS

10 1/2 oz. (300 g) **sedanini** or penne
2 1/2 oz. (70 g) **raisins** or golden raisins
3 1/2 oz. (100 g) **sliced almonds**, toasted (1 1/3 cups)
2 **green apples** (with peels)
3/4 cup (20 g) **chopped fresh parsley**
1/3 cup (80 ml) **extra-virgin olive oil**
*Juice of 1 **lemon***
Salt and pepper *to taste*

Boil the pasta in a pot of salted water until al dente. Remove from heat and quickly rinse under cold running water; drain carefully. Transfer to a large bowl and toss with a drizzle of olive oil so it does not stick together.
Soak the raisins in water for 10 to 15 minutes to plump them.
Drain well and squeeze gently. Slice (or cube) the apples and place in a bowl.
Add lemon juice and toss to coat apples.
Drain the lemon juice from the apples and whisk the juice with the olive oil, parsley and a pinch of salt and pepper; set aside. Mix the pasta with the apples, raisins and three-quarters of the almonds. Drizzle pasta with dressing and toss.
Serve on individual bowls or plates and garnish with remaining almonds.

INGREDIENTS INDEX

PHOTO CREDITS

All photographs are by ACADEMIA BARILLA except the following:
pages 6, 95 ©123RF

· · · · · · · · · · · ·

Original edition © 2013 by De Agostini Libri S.p.A.

The Taunton Press
Inspiration for hands-on living®

The Taunton Press, Inc.
63 South Main Street
PO Box 5506, Newtown, CT 06470-5506
e-mail: tp@taunton.com

Translations:
Catherine Howard - Mary Doyle - John Venerella - Free z'be, Paris
Salvatore Ciolfi - Rosetta Translations SARL - Rosetta Translations SARL

LIBRARY OF CONGRESS CATALOGING-IN-PUBLICATION DATA IN PROGRESS
ISBN: 978-1-62710-051-9

Printed in China
10 9 8 7 6 5 4 3 2 1